Psychic M

The Ultimate Guide to Psychic Abilities, Mediumship, and Astral Projection; How to Develop Clairvoyance, Connect with The Archangels, and Contact Your Spirit Guides.

MELISSA SMITH

INTRODUCTION

Have you ever felt like there's something more to you?

Do you sometimes feel as though another person is living inside you, who doesn't get a say in your life?

Do you have a knack for knowing what people are thinking?

Are you always able to sense when something bad is about to happen?

If you've answered yes to any of the above, you might be a psychic in the making

Psychic abilities can be a mysterious and feeling-filled realm for many people. But, if you're reading this, you probably already know that there's something about you that makes you feel more connected to your intuition than the average person. This is because having psychic abilities is natural and something most people possess to some extent. However, before you can develop your psychic abilities to the fullest, it's important to know where they come from and how to cultivate them.

When people think of someone who is psychic, they often imagine a person who can see into the future or know things that they couldn't possibly know just by using their five senses. While this is definitely one type of psychic ability, it's not the only one. In fact, there are many different types of psychic abilities, and not all of them involve seeing into the future.

Each of these abilities can be used to help you in your everyday life, whether it is to help you better understand a situation or to help you make a decision that will improve your life.

Most people think of these various psychic abilities as independent entities, but in reality, they are all interconnected. To tap into all of these various powers, a person must have a strong and healthy connection with his or her inner guidance system.

Developing your psychic abilities can be a daunting task, but it can also be inspiring, fun, and rewarding. Give yourself a realistic and positive outlook, and you'll be on your way to developing your abilities. When you learn how to use them, you begin to develop more insights about yourself and others. You start understanding the hidden meanings behind things, the reasons for why things happen, and the connections between people.

The development of a psychic ability requires practice, discipline, and patience. And while there are no clear-cut steps that you should follow, there are some general guidelines you can use to develop your power.

If you're ready to enter this magical world and explore your inner self, read on to learn more.

BECOME MORE IN TUNE WITH YOURSELF

There are some things in this world that we cannot know for sure. Some things have to be left to faith and intuition. These are the things we call "secrets".

But what if we could know for sure? What if we could rely on something other than our instincts? What if there was a way to contact the Source and get answers to the most important questions of our lives?

That's the premise for the world of mediumship, a spiritual practice that involves channeling visions from other dimensions. But is this something you can do? Are mediums real and not just myths or legends? What is the process for becoming a psychic? And how does it actually work?

Many people don't realize that they have psychic abilities. These abilities can manifest in a variety of ways, from feeling someone's emotions to seeing the future. Whether you're simply intuitive or you see full-blown visions, we all have a connection to the spiritual realm. If you're looking to tap into your abilities, there are a few things you can do to become more in tune with yourself.

First, start paying attention to your dreams. Dreams are often symbolic and can give you insight into your unconscious mind.

Keep a dream journal and write down any memorable dreams you have. As you journal, pay attention to any patterns or themes that emerge.

Also, be open to signs from the universe. This could be a song that keeps playing on the radio or a phrase you see multiple times throughout the day.

These signs are meant to guide and inspire you, so pay attention to what they're trying to tell you. Lastly, don't be afraid to experiment with divination tools like pendulums and crystal balls. These can help you gain clarity and receive messages from your higher self.

The difference between Psychics and Mediums

A psychic is someone who has the ability to use extrasensory perceptions to identify information that is not accessible to normal senses. This includes abilities such as: perceiving events that have not yet occurred, reading people's thoughts, or feeling the energy of places. A medium, on the other hand, is someone who acts as a conduit between the physical world and the spirit world. Mediums can channel spirits and communicate messages from the beyond. While both psychics and mediums have paranormal abilities, there is a key difference between the two: psychics do not necessarily believe that they are communicating with spirits, while mediums do. This is what sets them apart.

What if I told you, though, that you could be a psychic and a medium? A psychic medium is someone who possesses both psychic and mediumistic abilities. In other words, they can receive information from both the living and the dead. If you think you may be a Psychic Medium, there are certain signs to look for:

-You have frequent vivid dreams.

-You often have a strong sense of intuition or knowing.

-You are often able to see beyond the physical world

- You can pick up on the emotions or thoughts of others around you.

- You have a strong connection to nature or animals and can sense what they are feeling or experiencing.

-You know what people are thinking about even before they say it out loud

- You find yourself drawn to photographs or objects that belonged to someone who has passed away

-You can change someone's mood just by looking at them

-You can control your dreams

-You sense when someone is trying to read your mind

-You experience vivid visions of the future or past, which seem to have no rational explanation.

-You have sudden and unexplainable changes in behavior or emotional state.

-You find yourself drawn to certain people or places for no apparent reason.

-You frequently have déjà vu experiences.

- You frequently have dreams or premonitions about people who have died

-You have an increased interest in psychic abilities and the paranormal

If you recognize yourself in any of the above sentences, it is worth exploring further.

HOW TO BECOME A PSYCHIC MEDIUM

There is no one-size-fits-all answer to this question. However, there are a few things you can do to become a Psychic Medium. First and foremost, you need to have a willingness to explore the unknown. This means that you have to let go of what you know about yourself and the world around you. If you're not open to the idea of exploring your spiritual potential, then chances are you won't be able to access your power. Another important step is to develop strong relationships with other people who share similar interests or experiences within the spiritual realm. These relationships will allow you to build trust and access information that may be difficult for you to find on your own.

With patience and dedication, you can begin to see beyond the physical world and into the world of energy and spirits.

Becoming a psychic medium is no easy feat. It requires years of study and practice to develop the ability to communicate with the dead. However, for those who are willing to put in the work, it can be an incredibly rewarding experience. Here are some tips to help you on your journey to becoming a psychic medium:

1. Study the field of parapsychology. To become a psychic medium, you need to have a strong understanding of the paranormal.

2. Practice meditation and visualization techniques. To open your mind and tap into your psychic abilities, it's important to clear your thoughts and focus your energy.

Meditation and visualization can help you achieve this state of mind.

3. Attend a development circle. Development circles are groups that meet regularly to practice communicating with the dead. This is a great way to gain experience and learn from more experienced psychic mediums.

4. Be patient. Becoming a psychic medium takes time, patience, and practice. Don't get discouraged if you don't see results immediately - trust that with time and effort, you will develop your abilities.

5. Be aware of your limits. When you are working as a psychic medium, you will be dealing with energies that are much higher than your own. This can be very taxing on your physical and emotional bodies. It is important to know your limits and to take breaks when you need to.

6. Learn how to protect yourself from negative energy. When you are working as a psychic medium, you will be open to receiving energy from both the spirit world and the physical world. This can sometimes be overwhelming, so it is important to learn how to create a shield of positive energy around yourself. This will protect you from any negative energy that may try to attach itself to you.

7. Have a support system in place. When you are working as a psychic medium, you will be open to a lot of criticism. It is important to have a support system in place, such as family and friends, who will be there to support you.

CLAIRVOYANCE

Clairvoyance is the ability to see things that are not currently visible to the senses. Clairvoyance can be general and/or specific.

General clairvoyance is the ability to see and know everything at once as if you were looking through a window.

Specific clairvoyance is the ability to have one-on-one contact with someone that you don't know very well, like a loved one who has passed away.

The majority of clairvoyants experience visions of some form, but it is also not uncommon to receive non-visual information such as sounds, smells, or physical sensations. This Clair is also known as visual telepathy (or "seeing with the mind's eye'), a reference to the idea that clairvoyants see with their minds, not their eyes. While clairvoyance is most commonly associated with the ability to see visions in the form of images generated by the mind, it is also sometimes referred to as "clear sight", or "clear seeing because clairvoyants see things as they truly are, as opposed to seeing them through the filter of their own emotions and beliefs.

Clairvoyants have a "detached" sense of perception, in addition to a heightened level of awareness and observation. Recent research suggests that clairvoyants have a "split identity," with a part of their consciousness separated from their physical body. This allows them to perceive information that is not available to the five senses. In some cases, this extra-sensory perception can provide invaluable insights into the lives of others. For instance, clairvoyants have been known to help solve crimes and locate missing persons.

The phenomenon of clairvoyance has been a source of fascination for centuries. And while there is still much mystery surrounding this ability, scientists have begun to unlock some of the secrets of the mind's eye. The mind's eye is a part of the consciousness separated from the physical body: clairvoyants have a "split identity", in that they can access information stored in their mind's eye and project that information onto physical items receive. For example, clairvoyants may receive a vision of the future and project this vision into the physical object of a crystal or gem, in this case, the physical body acts as an amplifier for the mind's eye, and the object acts as a receiver for the mind's eye

The mind's eye is located in the cortex, the part of the brain responsible for visual processing. This theory is supported by studies of people who have sustained damage to their cortex - they often report losing their ability to see mental images. Additionally, neuroimaging techniques have shown that the same areas of the brain are activated when someone is viewing a physical object and when they are imagining that same object. This finding has important implications for our understanding of human consciousness – and it raises intriguing questions about the nature of reality itself. Are we living in one reality, or are there other realities that we can access through our minds? Only further research will yield the answer – but in the meantime, the mind's eye remains a tantalizing mystery.

There are three types of clairvoyance: precognition, the ability to perceive or predict future events; retrocognition, the ability to see past events; remote viewing, the perception of contemporary events happening outside of your range.

PRECOGNITION

Precognition is the ability to perceive events that have not yet taken place this ability has fascinated humans for thousands of years, and it can still be a subject of great debate and research today.

One of the most famous premonitions in history is that of Abraham Lincoln. According to reports, shortly before his death at the hands of John Wilkes Booth, Lincoln experienced several vivid dreams and hallucinations. In one dream, he saw his own body lying in a casket in the East Room of the White House. Lincoln woke up from the dream feeling very disturbed and told his wife, Mary Todd Lincoln, about it. Just a few days later, Booth fatally shot Lincoln while he was watching a play at Ford's Theatre. Today, many historians believe that Lincoln's premonitions were a result of his heightened awareness and intuition, as he was known to be a very intuitive and insightful man. Whatever the case may be, Lincoln's premonitions are certainly one of the most fascinating examples of psychic ability in history.

There are many ways you can learn to become a better precog, and you don't need to be a Tarot card reader or a crystal ball gazer to become more aware of your future. The most important thing is to pay attention, and that's exactly what you need to do to improve your chances of having precognitive experiences. It's important to note that precognition doesn't always mean the ability to perceive future events, It could also be the ability to perceive your thoughts or emotions before they occur, this can be very useful in understanding your emotions and how they relate to your life, but it is not a cure-all for your problems. Precognition is simply a tool that can help you see the bigger picture

Practice mindfulness

By practicing mindfulness, you will learn how to be in the moment and become more aware of your thoughts and actions. This is what will make it easier for you to notice small changes in your day-to-day life that could mean an event on the horizon. For example, if something doesn't feel right, pay attention. Maybe someone has been saying something negative about you or there was an argument with your co-worker at work. Pay attention and reflect on what these events might mean and what they can cause in the future.

Get out in nature

Another way you can improve your chances of having precognitive experiences is by spending time in nature. As you get lost in nature, you will be less focused on what's happening around you, which will help break down the barriers between your conscious and subconscious mind and allow messages from your future self to come through more easily. This could also potentially improve your mental health as well as your overall mood. As you spend time in nature, notice all the different sights and sounds that come along with it - this will help train your senses for what's going to happen next!

Practice Tasseography

Tasseography also known as tasseomancy or tea leaf reading is the art of reading symbols and messages left in the tea leaves. This practice is based on the belief that tea leaves have a spirit and can reveal hidden information and events that have yet to happen. Tasseomancy is not a new practice; in fact, it has been around for centuries throughout many cultures including China, Greece, India, Egypt, Pakistan, Africa, and even Europe where it was used by fortune-tellers as well by many witches during the Middle Ages.

Whether you are seeking guidance, insight, or simply want to explore the messages from your tea leaves, tasseomancy is a fun and unique way to gain a deeper understanding of yourself and your life path.

1. Make a cup of tea using loose-leaf tea and boiling water, being sure to focus your thoughts on the question or issue you would like premonitions about.

2. Pour hot water over the tea leaves, and allow them to steep for several minutes until the liquid turns dark in color.

3. Carefully pour out the liquid without disturbing the leaves at the bottom of the cup, then take a look at what patterns and shapes are formed in your tea leaves.

The symbols you see in your cup of tea will be unique to you and your specific situation. With that said, some general guidelines can be followed to get a better understanding of what the tea leaves are trying to tell you.

Clouds in the cup represent bad news or difficulties on the horizon.

Flowers are new beginnings or happy news.

A spider signifies a tangle of messes or a difficult circumstance.

A ship could symbolize a trip or new adventure.

A ring around the cup represents marriage or a commitment.

A key is something that was previously hidden and is now revealed.

A heart symbol might represent love or happiness.

A crossed-out symbol could represent an obstacle that needs to be overcome.

A thunderbolt could represent power or energy.

A spiral represents growth or change.

A triangle represents balance or harmony.

4. Record any premonitions that you see in your tea leaves, along with any other observations or insights you received.

While it's important to learn about your precognitive abilities, it's also important to know when to seek professional help. If you are experiencing increasing anxiety about having a vision or feeling that something is going to happen, you might want to see a professional.

RETROCOGNITION

Retrocognition refers to the ability to access memories, either through past-life regression or other forms of visualization and deep concentration. This process can be used to gain insight into past experiences that are affecting you in the present, as well as to connect with your higher self or spirit guides for guidance and healing.

This ability has been documented for centuries and can be traced back to the ancient Egyptians. The first recorded case of retrocognition was in 1806 by Jean-Martin Charcot who studied a woman who believed she had lived 100 years earlier. The woman's parents could not believe their daughter claimed to remember life before they were born, but she proved it through her knowledge of events that happened between then and now.

Most people think retrocognition is a ghostly ability that involves vanishing Victorian ladies walking in the corner of your eye or orbs of light floating around. While that's true in some cases, it's wrong to assume that.

In reality, retrocognition is much more subtle and sophisticated than that. It involves first a clear vision of your present surroundings, then a hazy vision or shroud covering your actual vision for about 3 - 7 seconds. During that brief time, your brain suddenly activates areas it usually doesn't, like the visual part of your dorsal visual stream. The result is that the information you are receiving through your usual senses is suddenly augmented with information received through your subconscious memory.

There are many benefits to retrocognition, including increased self-awareness, healing of past traumas, and gaining deeper insight into your purpose and life path. Some people also report experiencing a sense of peace or wholeness after accessing past-life memories, as well as a greater connection with their spirituality or intuition. Retrocognition can be a powerful tool for personal growth and transformation, as it can help you to release old patterns and beliefs that no longer serve you.

When you connect to your past lives, you're tapping into a wealth of information you can use to shift your current mindset. You can go further now than you ever have before in understanding your current life and how it relates to your previous lives

Past-life Regression

For obvious reasons, it will be difficult for you to have clear mental pictures if your mind and body are not relaxed enough by either slowing down consciously with long breaths or other stress-relieving mind frames

Before beginning your session, make sure you are clear about what you want to get out of it. You may find yourself asking questions about your past lives or getting clarity on certain issues from that life. You may want to explore why there are certain patterns or challenges in your current life that appear as if they came from your past life.

Once you feel ready, close your eyes and relax into a state of deep restfulness. The breath will become deeper and calmer until your mind becomes completely stilled and all thoughts have ceased. This is called a trance state, which will allow you to enter into deep sleep without any stress or fear present to connect with your past-life memories more easily

You can induce this trance state through breathing exercises, visualization, or simply by engaging in self-hypnosis. Once you start to enter the trance state, you will begin to feel a detachment from your everyday thoughts and worries, which will allow you to connect with your subconscious mind and past-life memories more easily. You will also begin to feel a deep sense of relaxation, which will allow your mind to wander and search for any previous-life memories that you may have.

This deep state of relaxation will create new neural pathways While you are in this trance state, you should be actively picturing how it felt to experience the memory in the past. This will allow you to access the memory much easier and it will also create a memory file in your brain so that the next time you want to access that memory, it will be much easier for your brain to recognize it.

Start with the basics: explore your personal beliefs and values before delving into the past life search process. Pick the right topic for what you're looking for. Some people choose to explore their family lineage or ancestral history, while others want to learn more about their purpose in life.

1. Start to imagine yourself floating in a river. The river represents time, and all of your past lives are represented by different points on the river.
2. Next, visualize yourself slowly moving backward in time along the river. As you continue to move backward, you begin to experience past life memories or visions of past lives. These memories may be vague

at first, but as you keep moving back through time, they will become clearer and more detailed.

3. When you find a past life that interests you, focus all of your attention on it. Try to recall specific details about this past life: who you were, where you lived, and what your goals and struggles were. You may also try interacting with other people from this past life, such as family members or friends.

One of the most important things to remember when interpreting past-life memories is that they are not always literal. Often, past-life memories will contain symbolic messages or lessons that you can apply to your current life. For example, if you have a past-life memory of being abandoned in a forest, this may symbolize feelings of isolation or loneliness that you are currently experiencing. Alternatively, if you have a past-life memory of being betrayed by a friend, this may represent a current situation in which you feel like you can't trust anyone.

Keep in mind that a past-life regression does not occur in a vacuum. You may still be susceptible to the same life challenges and issues that you experienced during your past lives.

A common goal for spiritual seekers is to understand how to become less attached to material possessions so that they can focus on what's truly important: their relationships. Past-life regression can help them achieve this goal by helping them understand that by owning less, they can spend more time focusing on the people who are important in their lives and what matters most to them.

Another goa something as simple as understanding why certain habits or actions of yours don't work out well for you. Maybe you eat way too much sugar but it never seems to be satisfying because you have no idea why that happens and what you could do differently next time. Or maybe you've tried countless diets over the years and they always seem to fail because no matter what diet plan you try, your cravings return quickly.

This all sounds like an easy fix on paper; just regress into one of your past lives when food was scarce and then learn how to find satisfaction again when it comes to food somehow? In reality, that's not so easy! Regression has its downsides too. Your conscious mind will try its best to interfere with the process if it perceives a threat, that's why you should consider finding a qualified practitioner who can guide you through the process and help you understand what you might be uncovering.

If you continue to work on healing your soul and your heart, you will find yourself with a much clearer message and purpose in your life!

REMOTE VIEWING

Remote viewing is a process that uses the power of the mind to obtain information about otherwise concealed or unknown objects, people, places, or events.

Remote viewing has been documented since its inception in the 1950s and has since been explored by researchers in many countries. While the majority of these studies have been conducted with a focus on the military, this does not mean that the practice cannot be applied to self-improvement or spiritual growth.

To take advantage of the practice of remote viewing, you will first need to learn how to connect to your higher self. This can be done through daily meditation and visualization exercises. As you improve your mental and spiritual connection, your remote viewing skills will also improve.

To create the most powerful remote viewing sessions, you need to set your intention.

What do you want to explore?

What do you want to learn? '

Set your intention as you begin to close your eyes, and feel the energy of the universe moving through your body.

Setting your intention will help you to focus your mind and create the right energy for your session. It will also help to keep you motivated as you explore your mind. You can use guided imagery to heighten your remote viewing experience. Visualizing what your remote viewing target looks like will help you to connect with the person or place you want to contact more easily.

You can use imaginary scenes or make up a story about the location, the more detail you can add to your visualization, the more likely you are to succeed. For example, you can start by imagining yourself standing in a field of tall grass. Then, take a few steps forward, and see yourself walking through the field. As you walk, feel the grass between your toes, smell the scents in the air, and hear the crickets chirping. By actively imagining the remote viewing experience, you'll heighten your chances of actually receiving information.

See yourself in a new situation, observe something new, or hear something new. As you explore the unknown, you are taking your conscious awareness to another dimension.

The basic idea is to try to sense or describe a location that you have never been to before, without using any conventional means of Gathering information. Try to describe the layout of a city that you have never visited or the interior of a building that you have never been inside. To maximize your chances of success, it is important to go into the exercise with an open mind and allow your intuition to guide you.

CLAIRCOGNIZANCE

Claircognizance is a type of extrasensory perception, that is characterized by a strong intuitive sense of knowing something without actually being able to explain or justify why you know it. Unlike clairvoyance, claircognizance often comes unexpectedly and seemingly out of nowhere and is more difficult to develop and train. However, with practice and dedication, claircognizance can be cultivated and honed over time, allowing you to tap into your intuition in powerful ways.

One common misconception about claircognizance is that it is just "gut instinct" or a form of "instinctive knowing." While the two may overlap at times, they are quite different. Gut instinct refers to a feeling or hunch based on past experience or pattern recognition, while claircognizance is a direct knowing that does not always have a logical explanation.

If you want to develop your claircognizant abilities, there are a few things you can do to get started. First, it is important to quiet the mind and allow yourself to be open to new information. This can be done through meditation, journaling, or any activity that allows you to clear your mind and focus inward. Once you have stilled the mind, begin to pay attention to any thoughts, feelings, or impulses that come up for you. These may come in the form of images, words, or just a sense of knowing. Trust whatever comes up for you, even if it doesn't make logical sense.

A useful technique for developing claircognizance is to engage in activities that require pattern recognition or intuitive thinking. This could involve trying your hand at things like

Tarot reading, astrology, palm reading, or any other activity that requires you to interpret symbolic information; you can also try engaging in activities like logic puzzles, riddles, or Sudoku games – anything that requires you to think outside the box and use your innate ability to see patterns and make connections.

Crystals are another tool that can be used to improve your claircognizance. Each crystal has its unique energy and vibration that can help to raise our consciousness and attune us to higher frequencies.

Here are a few examples of crystals that could be used to help develop or enhance claircognizance:

- **Clear quartz** is one of the most versatile and well-known crystals. It can be used for a variety of purposes, including amplifying energy, helping to cleanse the body of negative energy, and increasing clarity and focus. Clear quartz help opens up the mind to receive psychic information.

- **Citrine** is another crystal that is often associated with claircognizance. This yellow-colored stone help stimulate the mind and increase mental clarity and creativity which could help come up with new ideas or solutions.

- **Amethyst** is a beautiful violet-colored crystal that has a calming effect on the mind. This can be helpful in opening up to claircognizant experiences, as it can help to still the mind and allow for greater focus. Amethyst also protects against negative energy and psychic attack.

- **Moonstone** is a beautiful, translucent stone that comes in a variety of colors. It is named for its moon-like appearance, as the surface of the stone seems to shimmer and change when viewed from different angles. Moonstone is connected to the moon and its energies, which makes it an ideal crystal for those seeking psychic insights and guidance.

By regularly practicing claircognizance, you will gradually develop stronger intuitive skills and learn how to better trust your inner knowing!

CLAIRGUSTANCE

Clairgustance is the ability to taste or smell a substance without having it physically present. It is a form of extrasensory perception (ESP) that is sometimes also referred to as remote tasting or remote smelling. For example, someone might be able to taste the fear of another person or smell the memory of a particular place.

Clairgustance can be used for personal spiritual development and growth. For example, you may use clairgustance to taste the energy of different foods and beverages before you consume them, to determine which are healthiest for you. Or, you may use clairgustance to taste the energy of different people and places, to determine whether or not they are safe for you to be around.

Mindful eating is a term that is used to describe a type of eating that is based on awareness and attention. Mindful eating involves being present with our food, observing how it tastes and smells, how it feels in our bodies, and how we are feeling while eating.

While intuitive eating and clairgustance may seem very different, they are closely connected. Intuitive eating involves trusting our inner wisdom to make decisions about food and our health, while clairgustance helps us tune in to the subtle tastes and smells associated with emotions and energy. Both of these skills can be used to help us understand ourselves better and make more informed choices in our lives.

When you are eating, take a moment to focus on the food in front of you. Let yourself get lost in the experience of eating.

When you are finished, take a few minutes to reflect on how the food made you feel.

Start by studying the sense of taste. What are the different flavors that you can taste? What are the different sensations that you feel when you taste something?

Imagine that you can taste things from a distance, such as the aroma of a flower or the flavor of another person's feelings.

One way to refine your clairgustance skills is to experiment with different types of food. Try new flavors, textures, and smells. By expanding your culinary horizons, you will be able to better understand the emotions and the energies behind the different tastes.

CLAIRTANGENCY

Have you ever gone to a garage sale and picked up an old piece of furniture, only to have strange memories or feelings come into your mind? If so, you may have experienced clairtangency, also known as psychometry.

Everyone knows there's a reason why people keep old family photos, jewelry, and other personal mementos. These objects give people a sense of connection to the past, the people they love and the places they've lived. They also serve as a kind of psychic record of positive and negative personal experiences that can be used to uncover past traumas, habits, or other issues that might affect a person's present behavior.

Psychometry is the ability to experience or sense something through an inanimate object. It is the act of reading information from an object by 'touching' it with your 'soul'. You can use a photo, a table, a map, a book, or anything that you feel can give you a 'reading'. You just need to be in tune with the object and the energy that it emanates and gain information about the past, present, or future. It can be used to find out about people who have passed away, people who are still alive, or even to connect with your past life or receive guidance for your current situation.

There are two types of psychometry: direct and indirect. Direct psychometry occurs when the viewer learns about an object by coming into contact with it. Indirect psychometry, on the other hand, occurs when the viewer gains information about an object without coming

Begin by choosing an object that holds a meaningful connection for you. It can be anything from a photograph of a loved one to a favorite book or piece of jewelry. Once you've selected your object, start asking yourself:

"What does this object represent?"

"Who has touched this object?"

"What do I feel when I hold this object?"

Take the object and hold it close to your heart.

Hold the object up to a window or light source for twenty seconds without letting go.

Plant your hands on top of the object and ask if there is anything from its past or present that would like to share with you.

You can now start asking questions, or simply be open to what you receive. Be sure to record any messages, insights, or ideas that come to you.

Keep in mind that even though your object is not alive, it still has a consciousness, and it can tap into different dimensions to assist you in your journey. It's important to maintain an open mind and be receptive to new information. You may also find it useful to journal or share your journey with a supportive person.

Once you've finished connecting with your object, let it go. It doesn't need to stay with you. It doesn't need to be "saved" or "attached" to you. It simply is, and now you can connect with it whenever you wish.

TELEPATHY

Telepathy is the act of communicating mentally with another person without physically interacting. Whether you are trying to communicate with your boss, your best friend, or your lover, telepathy can help you get your message across.

The word comes from the Greek tele, meaning "far," and pathe, meaning "feeling, perception, or suffering." It means "far-feeling." The term was first coined in the late 19th century by psychologist Frederic Myers, and he defined it as "the communication of impressions of any kind from one mind to another, without the use of any recognized physical means."

Aristotle described telepathy as a type of "divine madness" and believed that it was an ability found only in the Gods. He believed that this ability was responsible for their ability to know what was going on in the minds of humans.

Throughout history, there have been countless stories and accounts of people displaying telepathic ability. Perhaps the most famous example comes from Ancient Greece, with the story of Odysseus and his son Telemachus. As the legend goes, Odysseus was away at war for twenty years, during which time his wife Penelope was besieged by suitors who hoped to marry her and claim Odysseus's kingdom. One day, Penelope had a dream in which Odysseus appeared to her and told her to be patient - he would soon return home. The very next day, Telemachus had a similar dream in which he saw his father and was warned of the danger that Penelope was in. Inspired by their dreams, both Odysseus and Telemachus took decisive action that led to the destruction of the suitors and the reunion of the family. Although this story is undoubtedly mythical, it speaks to the power of telepathic connection between loved ones who are far apart.

Many people have an innate desire to understand what other people are thinking and feeling. And for good reason – telepathy and mind-reading can be powerful tools for building stronger relationships, improving communications skills, and even revealing hidden insights about ourselves and others. But how can we learn to telepathically communicate with others?

Here are some tips and exercises to help develop your telepathic abilities.

1. **Pay attention to your dreams.**

   Dreams can be powerful sources of information, and often contain messages from our subconscious minds. Keep a dream journal by your bed and make a note of any dreams that stand out to you – especially those that seem to contain messages or symbols that you don't understand. Over time, you may start to see patterns emerge that can help you interpret the dream messages you receive.

2. Practice visualization exercises.

One of the best ways to develop telepathic abilities is to practice "sending" images and thoughts to another person.

Find a quiet place to sit or lie down and relax your whole body.

Once you're physically and mentally calm, visualize a clear message that you want to convey to your partner. Try to focus on the exact words or images that you wish to send – this will help train your mind in the art of telepathic communication.

Take a few deep breaths and clear your mind of all thoughts.

Visualize yourself going inside his/her mind

Try picturing the scene from their perspective instead of yours

Focus your attention on what they are thinking or feeling

As you start to receive images or words, write them down.

Compare your results with your partner to see how accurate you were.

CLAIRSENTIENCE

Clairsentience simply means 'clear feeling' – the ability to clearly feel the energy. It is the capacity to perceive and experience the energetic vibration of anything, inside and out. It is the awareness of the energetic dimensions of reality, and how things and people affect us

Clairsentience is one of the most powerful gifts that we can possess. It allows us to see beyond the physical world and into the energetic dimensions of reality. With clairsentience, we can perceive the vibrational energy of all things, both inside and outside of ourselves. This awareness enables us to understand how different people and things can affect our energy field. Clairsentience is an invaluable tool for anyone who wishes to create a more balanced and healthier lifestyle. By understanding the energetic vibration of our food, our thoughts, and our environment, we can make choices that will lead to a more wholesome and fulfilling life.

Everything has an energetic fingerprint, and clairsentience is the ability to perceive these signatures. Everything has a frequency, and clairsentience is the ability to resonate at that frequency. It is the awareness of how we can make things better for ourselves, our loved ones, our community, or society as a whole. The world would be a much better place if everyone had clairsentience.

To understand what clairsentience means, you need to understand what empathy means too – because empathy and clairsentience are closely related concepts (and often confused with each other). When someone experiences empathy, they have an empathic response to the thoughts, feelings, and emotions of another person. When someone experiences clairsentience, they have an empathic response to the thoughts, feelings, and emotions of another person that is so powerful that it enables them to gain access to those people's memories, perceptions, and experiences.

Empathy and clairsentience are both extremely useful when it comes to improving our relationships with other people – especially our relationships with our family members, friends, and romantic partners.

If empathy enables us to feel what others feel for us to better understand them, clairsentience enables us to gain access to other peoples' memories and perceptions so that we can learn from their experiences without actually having those experiences ourselves – which often helps us get along better with them in the long run too.

Look at people, places, and things with a fresh eye - be aware of their energetic field. Notice how you are affected by different types of people by either having an emotional reaction or being neutral to them. Some people will have a more negative energetic field than others. Be aware of which ones you tend to gravitate to or avoid. The more you practice this daily self-exam, the more familiar you become with how your body feels in different situations.

CHAKRAS

Chakra is a Sanskrit word that means "wheel" or "turning". The chakras are the seven main energy centers of the body. Each one is located along the spine, from the base of the spine to the crown of the head and each one is associated with a different aspect of our physical, emotional, and spiritual selves.

The chakras are responsible for distributing energy throughout the body and keeping everything in balance. As we go through life, our chakras can become blocked or out of balance, if one of the chakras is out of alignment, it can cause physical, mental, or emotional problems, consequently, it is important for psychics to be aware of the chakras and to keep them in balance. By keeping them in balance, we can maintain our health and well-being, be more effective in our work and prevent ourselves from becoming overloaded with energy, which can lead to burnout.

The seven chakras are:

• **The root chakra** (located at the base of the spine) is responsible for our sense of safety and security. It helps us feel grounded and connected to our bodies. When this chakra is out of balance, we may feel anxious or fearful. To bring the root chakra into balance, we can practice meditation and other relaxation techniques. We can also eat grounding foods like root vegetables and drink plenty of water. By taking care of our root chakras, we can help to ensure that we are physically and emotionally stable.

• **The sacral chakra** (located just below the navel) is associated with the element of water and the color orange.

The main energy center of the sacral chakra is the pelvis, and it governs our reproductive organs and sexual vitality. If this chakra is out of balance, we may experience problems with fertility, creativity, or sexual expression. To keep this chakra in balance, we can practice yoga or breathwork. We can also eat foods that are orange in colors, such as carrots, oranges, and mangoes. By balancing our sacral chakra, we can maintain our creative flow and connect with our sexuality healthily.

- **The solar plexus chakra** (located above the navel) is responsible for our power and sense of self-worth. This chakra is ruled by the element of fire, and its color is yellow. When this chakra is in balance, we feel empowered and able to take control of our lives. We are able to set boundaries and stand up for ourselves. We also have a strong sense of self-worth and are able and receive love freely. However, when the solar plexus chakra is out of balance, we feel powerless, we have difficulty setting boundaries or standing up for ourselves.

If you feel like your solar plexus chakra is out of balance, there are several things you can do to restore balance. First, try meditating on the color yellow. Visualize a bright yellow sun shining down on you, infusing you with its power and warmth. You can also try eating yellow foods, such as yellow bell peppers or squash.

- **The heart chakra** (located in the center of the chest) is responsible for our ability to love and be loved. When this chakra is balanced, we feel confident and secure in our relationships. We can give and receive love freely, without attachment or fear. We feel compassion for others and ourselves, and we radiate warmth and kindness. However, when the heart chakra is imbalanced, we may experience feelings of jealousy, insecurity, and resentment. We have a hard time letting go of past hurt, or we may find it difficult to open up to new people. We may also experience physical symptoms such as chest pain or difficulty breathing. To restore balance to the heart chakra, we can focus on self-love and compassion.

If you suspect that your heart chakra is out of balance, there are a few simple things you can do to help restore harmony. Spend time in nature, practice acts of kindness, and meditate on qualities such as love, compassion, and forgiveness. By making a conscious effort to nurture your heart chakra, you can cultivate more peace and joy in your life.

- **The throat chakra** is the fifth chakra and is located at the base of the neck. This chakra is associated with communication, self-expression, and creativity. When this chakra is in balance, we are able to express ourselves clearly and confidently. We are also able to listen to others with empathy and understanding. However, when the throat chakra is out of balance, we may experience difficulty communicating our needs, feel like we are not being heard, or become tongue-tied. We may also find it hard to express our creative ideas. If your throat chakra is out of balance, there are a few things you can do to restore balance. First, try meditating on a blue crystal, such as sodalite or lapis lazuli. You can also try chanting or singing sacred sounds such as "OM." Finally, make sure to drink plenty of water to keep your body and mind hydrated. By restoring balance to your throat chakra, you will be able to better communicate your needs and express your creativity.
- **The third eye chakra** is located in the center of the forehead, just above the eyebrows. It is associated with the element of space and is responsible for our ability to see clearly,

both physically and intuitively. When this chakra is in balance, we have a strong sense of inner vision and intuition. We can see clearly both what is happening around us and what is happening within us. We are open to new ideas and perspectives, and we can think creatively and solve problems effectively. When the third eye chakra is out of balance, we may experience headaches, eyestrain, or difficulties with concentration. We may also find it difficult to trust our intuition or see clearly what is happening around us balancing this chakra can help us to see both the world and ourselves more clearly.

- **The crown chakra** is the seventh and highest chakra. It is located at the top of the head, above the fontanelle. The crown chakra is associated with wisdom, spiritual connection, and Divine guidance. When the crown chakra is open, we can receive and understand higher knowledge. We feel connected to a Higher Power and our intuition is strong. We know our true purpose in life and we can live in alignment with our highest potential. We feel joyful, peaceful, and fulfilled. We are open to new ideas and perspectives, and we are receptive to change. If the crown chakra is overactive, we may feel disconnected from reality, scatter-brained, and spacey. We may be prone to hallucinations and irrational thinking. When the crown chakra is blocked, we feel closed-minded, trapped in old patterns of thinking, and cut off from our spiritual connection. To balance the crown chakra, practice visualization, mantra recitation, yoga poses such as Headstand or Camel Pose, and aromatherapy with essential oils such as frankincense or sandalwood.

THIRD EYE AWAKENING

In Egyptian mythology, the third eye was associated with the god Horus. This all-seeing eye was said to provide wisdom and insight, and it was often depicted on the pharaoh's crown. The third eye was also thought to protect against evil spirits, and it played an important role in the process of mummification. In Hinduism, it is called the "Ajna Chakra" is considered to be the center of psychic power and It is symbolized by a dot in the middle of the forehead called "bindi" which is traditionally worn by Hindu women. The bindi is a symbol of Goddess Lakshmi and is a sign of good luck and protection.

The third eye is a small, cone-shaped gland located in the center of the brain also known as The Pineal Gland. This gland is responsible for secreting melatonin, a hormone that regulates the body's sleep-wake cycle. In addition, the third eye produces a chemical called P-hydroxy-DMT (P-hydroxy-DMT) a molecule that is similar to serotonin which plays an important role in regulating mood and influencing sexual behavior.

The third eye is a gateway to higher consciousness and understanding. It allows us to see things more clearly, both physically and spiritually. When the third eye is open, we are able to connect with our true selves and access our intuition and psychic abilities. It's a conduit for spiritual energy and works in conjunction with the Sacral and Solar plexus Chakras to enlighten the soul. It allows us to tune into different frequencies and dimensions that we are not normally aware of and receive information that we would not be able to access otherwise. We feel more connected to ourselves, our loved ones, and the universe as a whole.

On the other hand, a dormant third eye can cause psychic blindness, nightmares, and high levels of stress. We may experience confusion, doubt, and insecurity. We may find it difficult to trust our intuition and make decisions that are truly in our best interest.

The good news is the Third Eye can be awakened through spiritual practices.

To open the third eye, start by finding a comfortable place to sit or lie down.

Close your eyes and take a few deep breaths to relax your body and mind. Once you're feeling calm, visualize a bright light in front of you.

Imagine the light growing brighter and brighter until it fills your entire field of vision. You may feel a tingling sensation in your forehead as the third eye opens.

Keep visualizing the light until you feel fully connected to it. Then, allow your thoughts to flow freely and see what insights come to you. If you find it difficult to keep your mind focused, try focusing on your breath or repeating this mantra:

I am open to the wisdom of the universe.

I trust my intuition and listen to my inner voice.

I am connected to all that is.

I am one with the divine intelligence of the cosmos.

As I recite this mantra, I visualize a bright light shining from my third eye, expanding my consciousness and opening me up to new levels of understanding.

By opening my third eye, I am tapping into a vast storehouse of knowledge and Divine guidance.

I am accessing my highest potential and living in alignment with my soul's purpose.

The third eye is the gate that leads to inner worlds and higher dimensions of consciousness. By opening the third eye, we raise our vibration and become more attuned to our true nature. It's the key to unlocking our psychic abilities. Who knows what you will be able to see once your third eye is opened?

THE SPIRITUAL REALM

Mediumship can be a deeply transformative experience that can help us to connect with our higher power, guides, and departed loved ones. Through mediumship, we are able to tap into the wisdom and knowledge of these spiritual beings, gaining insights and guidance that we may not have otherwise been able to access. This can help us to navigate challenges in our lives more effectively, make better decisions, and live more fulfilling lives overall.

The history of mediumship can be traced back to ancient times when humans would seek guidance from the spirit world to gain insight into their lives and the world around them. Throughout history, there have been many famous mediums and channelers who have brought messages from the other side, including Helen Keller, Edgar Cayce, and Nostradamus.

Whether you are looking for guidance in your personal life or seeking answers to the big questions about the universe, mediumship can be a powerful tool for connecting with the other side.

There are many different types of spiritual entities, and each one can offer us different insights and guidance. Some of the most common types of spiritual entities include angels, spirit guides, departed loved ones, and spirit animals.

Angels are divine messengers who serve as protectors and guides. They often help to deliver messages from the other side, offering guidance and support in times of need. To connect with angels, it is important to have a strong sense of faith and believe in their presence.

Most people are familiar with the popular image of angels as benevolent beings with wings. However, there is much more to these divine creatures than meets the eye. Angels are powerful beings who serve as protectors and guides. To connect with angels, it is important to have a strong sense of faith and believe in their presence. There are several different varieties of angels, each with a distinct function.

- **Guardian angels** are perhaps the most well-known type of angel. They are assigned to each one of us to protect and guide us through our lives, offering guidance and support when we need it most. Many people believe that their guardian angel is with them always, providing support and strength in moments of adversity.
- **Archangels** are the most powerful angels in the spiritual realm and are responsible for helping to guide and protect humanity.

1. Archangel Michael is the archangel of strength, courage, and protection. He is known as the defender of the faith and the prince of angels.
2. Archangel Raphael is the archangel of healing and restoration. He is known as the angel of divine healing and peace.
3. Archangel Gabriel is the archangel of communication and inspiration. He is known as the messenger of God and the angel of revelation.

4. Archangel Uriel is the archangel of guidance and enlightenment. He is known as the angel of light and truth.
5. Archangel Zadkiel is the archangel of mercy and forgiveness. He is known as the angel of righteousness and justice
6. Archangel Jophiel is the archangel of beauty and harmony. She is known as the angel of wisdom and understanding.
7. Archangel Chamuel is the archangel of love and compassion. He is known as the angel of divine love and peace.

Each one of these archangels has a specific function, but they all work together to protect us and guide us on our journey through life and we can call on them for help when we need it most.

- **Healing angels** are devoted to helping us heal physically, emotionally, and spiritually.

Spirit Guides are spiritual beings who act as teachers and mentors on our earthly journey. They can help us to understand the lessons we are learning on our path, offer insight into difficult situations, and provide guidance when we are making important life decisions. It is believed that we each have one or more spirit guides who are assigned to us before we are born. These guides remain with us throughout our lives, offering their assistance and wisdom when needed. While they are always available to help us, it is up to us to listen to their guidance and follow their advice. In doing so, we can learn the lessons we need to to lead happy and fulfilling lives.

Ascended Masters are highly revered spiritual beings who have attained a high level of spiritual evolution. They are free from the cycle of birth and death and have achieved a state of enlightenment. They can travel back and forth between heaven and earth at will. One of the most well-known ascended masters is Jesus Christ. Other ascended masters include Buddha, Kuan Yin, Saint Germain, and Mother Mary. These beings are revered by many spiritual seekers as sources of wisdom, inspiration, and guidance. By following their teachings and working with them on a spiritual level, we can all aspire to achieve the highest level of spiritual evolution.

The ascended masters are a group of advanced spiritual beings who have dedicated their eternity to the primordial act of service to humanity and all of creation. They are our caregivers, our infinite supply of unconditional love and support, and are always with us even if we are not yet aware of them. The ascended masters have come from all walks of life, and every corner of the globe. They are ordinary people who have taken their God-given gifts and talents and used them in extraordinary ways to make a difference in the world. While they are no longer incarnate on the earth plane, they continue to serve as our guardians, teachers, and healers, providing us with guidance and wisdom when we need it most. The ascended masters are here to help us remember our true nature as divine beings and to assist us in our journey back to the Source.

Cherubs: are a type of angel that is often depicted as having a small, chubby body with wings and a halo. They are symbols of innocence and purity. The role of the cherubs is to act as messengers and helpers between God and man. They can help us by delivering prayers to God and bringing us messages from Him. Because of their close connection with God, they are very wise and powerful beings.

Seraphim are the highest-ranking angels and are often depicted as fiery six-winged beings. In Christianity, they are the caretakers of God's throne. The word "seraph" is derived from the Hebrew word for "burning," which is fitting given their fiery nature. They have multiple faces, which may explain why they are depicted as having many eyes in religious artworks. They are completely devoted to God and His will, and they work tirelessly to carry out His commands. They can also help us on a more personal level guiding and supporting us through tough times, offering strength and comfort.

Departed loved ones are those who have died but still maintain a connection to the physical world. They often visit us in our dreams or moments of meditation, offering love from the other side. In addition to providing comfort and guidance, these visits can also offer closure and understanding. For those who are grieving, connecting with a departed loved one can be an invaluable experience. Whether you are seeking to communicate with a specific individual or simply looking to connect with the spirit world, mediumship is a powerful tool. There is no greater gift than the ability to commune with the departed spirits of our loved ones. Though they may be gone from this world, we can bridge the divide.

Mediums can channel the energy of the departed and relay messages of love and guidance from the other side. This is a deeply personal experience that can offer tremendous comfort and healing. For those who have lost a loved one, mediumship can provide solace and reassurance that they are still very much a part of our lives. The connection we have with our departed loved ones is eternal, and we can keep the lines of communication open.

Spirit animals are powerful totems that offer us wisdom and guidance. They can help us to understand our emotions and instincts. By connecting with our spirit animal, we can deepen our understanding of our inner wisdom and intuition. In addition, it can be a powerful way to connect with the natural world and channel the energy of the earth

A Spirit animal represents your personality traits or characteristics. For example, if you are calm and collected you might have a turtle as your spirit animal, while those who are fiery and passionate might have a lion.

Here are some of the most common spirit animals and what they represent:

-Bear: strength, courage, Bear totem people are said to be natural healers with a deep connection to the earth. They are also known for their introspection and wisdom.

-Tiger: power, passion, People with a tiger spirit animal are confident and brave. They are known for their independent streak and their determination.

-Eagle: vision, truth, People with an eagle spirit animal are powerful and wise. They are known for their keen sense of observation and their ability to see the world from a different perspective.

-Wolf: loyalty, family, People with a wolf spirit animal are loyal and protective. They are known for their strong sense of community and their deep connection to nature.

There are many different ways to connect with your spirit animal. Some people dream of their animal guide, while others receive visions or visitations in meditation. Others may feel a sudden kinship with a certain species or find that they are repeatedly drawn to animals of a certain type. No matter how you come to recognize your spirit animal, there are a few key things to look for. First, pay attention to which animals you are naturally drawn. Animals that you feel a deep affinity for or fascination with are likely to be your spirit guides.

Secondly, take notice of the animals that appear in your dreams. These may be visitation from your animal guides and can give you important clues about their identity and meaning.

Lastly, be open to signals from the universe. Your spirit animal may make itself known in surprising ways, so always be on the lookout for unexpected encounters. By attuning yourself to these signs, you can begin to form a connection with the animal kingdom that will last a lifetime.

Trust your intuition and let yourself be guided to the animal that can help you on your journey.

CONTACTING THE SPIRIT WORLD

Find a quiet place where you won't be disturbed and turn off any electronic devices that are in the room.

Light three white candles and place them in a triangle shape on your altar (if you have one). If you don't have white candles, then you can use any other color instead, but white is best because it represents purity and innocence which is what we want when we invoke spirits!

Light some sandalwood incense sticks and place them to the left of the candles (if you are right-handed) or to the right of the candle (if you are left-handed).

Now say: *"I call upon the spirits of the air, earth, fire, water, and spirit to come to me in my circle and help me with my spell."* and *"I call upon the spirits of my ancestors to come forth and help me with my problem".*

Repeat the spell three times while visualizing a white light surrounding your body

Once you have said this, sit down and close your eyes again for a few minutes while meditating once more. This will help you focus on what is about to happen next. After doing this for a few minutes, open your eyes again and blow out all of the candles except one.

The first thing that you should do is ask the spirits if they are present and willing to communicate with you. If they are, then they will usually give some sort of indication that they are there such as making a noise or moving something in the room. If they aren't there, then it's best to wait until another time when they might be more willing to communicate.

Once the spirit has indicated that they are present and willing to communicate with you, then it's time for the real work of communicating with them to begin!

Ask them their name and where they come from. You should also ask them what their purpose is in contacting you at this time. Once this information has been gathered, then you can ask them any other questions that you might have.

Once you've finished communicating with the spirit, thank them for their time and let them know that they are free to go.

You can do this by saying something like *"Thank you for your time, I hope that we will meet again soon."*

Now it's best to leave the room and not talk about the experience until a few hours have passed. This is because spirits tend to stick around for a while after they have communicated.

Remember that channeling is a powerful spiritual practice that should be approached with care and reverence. While it can be a deeply transformative experience, it should always be approached with respect and responsibility.

1. Always be respectful to the channeled entity.

2. Ask for guidance and protection from your spiritual guides and higher power.

3. Be open and willing to receive information from the channeled entity.

4. Trust your intuition and pay close attention to any guidance or messages you receive during channeling sessions.

5. Seek professional help if you are experiencing any negative side effects from channeling, such as physical or emotional discomfort, anxiety, or confusion.

THE ASTRAL BODY

The astral body is the second layer of our being and connects the human body with our divine essence. The astral body and the soul are two very important parts of our being. While they are often confused, they are quite different. The astral body is made up of energy and is responsible for our emotions and thoughts. The soul, on the other hand, is the spiritual part of us that lives on after death. The astral body is a bridge between the spiritual realm and the material world, helping us to understand what makes us who we are.

The Aura is the manifestation of that bridge.

The Aura is a complex energy field that surrounds and permeates the human body. The chakras are connected to the aura and interact with it to maintain our health and well-being. By understanding the aura, we can learn to control and direct our energy field to create desired results in our lives. For example, if we want to attract more love into our lives, we can work on opening and balancing our heart chakra. If we want to improve our mental clarity, we can work on clearing and balancing our third chakra.

The aura is comprised of several layers, each of which has a specific purpose for the body and mind.

The Etheric Layer is the closest to the physical body and is responsible for our vitality and health. This layer vibrates at a very high frequency and is made up of prana, or life force energy. This energy is what keeps us alive and healthy. It contains information about our physical bodies, and it regulates all bodily functions such as heartbeat and respiration.

When this layer is out of balance, we experience physical health problems such as fatigue, illness, or pain. We may also find it difficult to connect with our spiritual selves.

The Emotional Layer governs our emotions and feelings. This layer vibrates at a low frequency and is made up of energy vibrations. This energy is what allows us to feel love, joy, sadness, and anger. The Emotional Layer stores all of our emotional memories and reactions. It affects how we feel on a day-to-day basis

The Mental Layer is where all of our thoughts and intellectual processes occur. It contains our memories, both conscious and subconscious. This layer vibrates at a medium frequency and is made up of thoughts and ideas. This energy is what allows us to think, learn, and create. When this layer is out of balance, we experience mental health problems such as anxiety, depression, or psychosis.

The Astral Layer is the place where we access our hopes, fears, and fantasies. This layer vibrates at an even higher frequency than the etheric layer and is responsible for our ability to feel passion, desire, and motivation. This body is also responsible for our psychic abilities and intuition. It governs our ability to connect with others emotionally and spiritually and allows us to experience other dimensions and planes of existence. It is the realm of dreams and fantasy, where we can explore new possibilities and explore the innermost recesses of our minds. When the astral layer is in balance, we can use our psychic abilities to their fullest potential!

The Etheric Template Body can be seen as a blueprint or pattern for the physical body. It contains all of the information needed to create a physical body, including DNA, genetic coding, and information about health and vitality and it is also responsible for transmitting information between the physical body and the other layers of the aura.

The Spiritual Template Layer governs our spiritual nature. It contains the blueprint for our soul and determines our life purpose. When the spiritual template layer is out of balance, it can lead to feelings of disconnection, confusion, and frustration.

The Causal Body Layer is the highest level of the spiritual body. It is a "template" for the perfect human form and contains all of the archetypes of human experience. This layer is the home of our soul and our spiritual identity it's our connection to the divine and guides our soul's journey. It helps us connect to a higher power and access our highest ideals and spiritual aspirations. The causal layer is the home of our soul and is responsible for our karma and destiny. It stores all of our past lives experiences and determines our future experiences.

AURA READING

Auras are a visual representation of a person's internal emotions and energy. They change constantly with our moods, thoughts, and feelings. It can also change based on what we wear or eat or drink! The color of our aura indicates if we are healthy or sick, happy or sad and it can even indicate how others feel about us. Many different types of aura colors can indicate different things about health, mental state, or personality traits.

<u>To see auras, you need to be able to tune into your energy and sense the energy of others.</u>

- *-Start by focusing on your breath.*
- *-Each time you inhale and exhale, check in with your breath and notice how your body feels.*
- *Use your peripheral vision. Gaze at a person's head and shoulders without looking directly at them. You may see a faint halo around their body or a bright outline of colors that change and shift.*

BLUE

A blue aura is a peaceful one that shows the mind and body are at peace. It is a sign of contentment, inner happiness, and wisdom. The blue aura is often associated with the element of water, which can help to show the connectedness between different people in a room. It shows that people in the room are friendly and open to new experiences. People with blue auras are often calm, compassionate, and caring. They are good at communication and relationships, and they have a strong connection to the natural world. Different shades of blue can indicate different qualities, such as wisdom (dark blue), peace (light blue), or truth (turquoise).

RED

A red aura shows anger, passion, or resentment and it can also indicate a feeling of danger or fear. The red aura is also commonly seen in people who constantly get annoyed by things that are said to them by others; a red aura also has positive meanings such as love, passion, safety, protection, and strength; a person with a red aura is passionate, driven, and confident. In general, people with red auras are natural leaders who are not afraid to take risks and go after what they want. A deep red aura indicates leadership ability, determination, and passion for success, A lighter red aura can indicate a more relaxed and easy-going personality, while a slightly pink aura may mean that the person is sensitive and artistic.

YELLOW

Yellow is the color of confidence and optimism. In nature, this color is seen in the rays of sunshine and symbolizes hope and cheerfulness. A yellow aura usually indicates joy, excitement, curiosity, and energy; however, it can also indicate conflict within the person's life. People with yellow auras are happy, creative, and intelligent. They tend to be optimistic, intuitive, and positive, and they're usually good at problem-solving.

Different shades of yellow can indicate a variety of qualities: a bright or golden yellow aura is associated with happiness and a sense of contentment. On the other hand, a pale- or lemon-yellow aura may indicate more anxious or stressed energy; a muddy or murky yellow aura is often associated with a lack of clarity or confusion.

GREEN

Green represents growth and regeneration. People with a green aura are ambitious and creative. They are likely to be very successful in their career or life in general. The green aura also means that they have good health and can recover from illness quickly.

There are many different types of green auras: people with a lime green aura are optimistic and enthusiastic individuals who approach life with enthusiasm and energy. Meanwhile, those with an olive-green aura are often seen as introverted and reserved, but also highly intelligent and creative individuals. A mint green aura represents new beginnings and hope. A forest green aura represents growth and abundance and it is associated with nature and fertility. Finally, an emerald green aura is associated with balance and kindness.

WHITE

A white aura is generally associated with purity, innocence, and light. People who have a white aura are kind and compassionate, as well as have a strong connection to their spiritual side. They may be highly intuitive or empathetic individuals, always striving to do good in the world. The white is associated with a divine nature, and is, therefore, an excellent indicator of spiritual power and is the result of an individual's faith or spirituality.

ORANGE

People with an orange aura are warm and friendly, but also outgoing and adventurous. They may be quick to start new projects and enjoy socializing but they usually have a short attention span. They are creative and spontaneous, but they may also be impulsive and reckless. Orange aura individuals are usually optimistic and full of energy, but they can also be impatient and easily bored. An orange aura can sometimes indicate that a person is feeling low in energy or is experiencing some degree of depression. If you see an orange aura around someone, it's important to be supportive and understanding - they may be going through a tough time.

VIOLET

A person with a violet aura is usually a wise and spiritual person. They tend to be very logical and analytical, and their thinking often revolves around deeper and more philosophical questions. They are usually quiet and reserved, and prefer to keep to themselves. They are extremely loyal and affectionate people, who cherish family and friends very highly, and are protective of those they care about.

Auras are a highly individualized energy system and should be viewed as a way to gain insight into the inner workings of a person's mind and emotions. Whether you're reading your aura or someone else's, you should pay close attention to the other colors present as well as the overall energy of the person to get a well-rounded reading.

Aura Cleansing

Negative thoughts can hurt your aura by creating dense, dark energy that can clog your energy field and prevent you from receiving positive energy. This can lead to feelings of fatigue, stress, and negativity, and can even hurt your physical health.

There are several things you can do to maintain a healthy aura.

✓ **Make sure to take time each day to relax and recharge your energy.** This can be done through activities like yoga, meditation, or simply taking a few moments to yourself each day.

✓ **Try to stay positive and optimistic!** When you are in a negative energy state, you are sending out the energy of resentment, which will be reflected at you. By consciously trying to send out positive energy, you can change your energy state and start to receive the energy of love and positivity back.

✓ **Aromatherapy is one of the best ways to keep our auras in check.** Lavender, rosemary, bergamot, frankincense, clary sage, and cypress are all excellent choices for maintaining a healthy aura. Lavender is particularly effective at calming and soothing the mind and body, while rosemary can help to refresh and revive the spirit. Bergamot is also known for its ability to purify and cleanse the aura, and frankincense is an excellent all-purpose option for protecting and balancing the aura. Clary sage has a rejuvenating effect that can help to lift the mood and promote mental clarity while cypress provides protection. When using any of these oils, be sure to use them in a diffuser or add them to your bathwater so that they can be evenly dispersed throughout your space. You can also add a few drops to a cotton ball and place it in your pillowcase so that you can enjoy their benefits while you sleep.

✓ **Music has a profound effect on the aura and can be used to help cleanse and purify it.** Certain types of music can work to raise the vibration of the aura. Avoid music with lyrics that are angry, violent, or depressing, as these can negatively affect the aura. Instead, try listening to music that is soothing and uplifting. Classical or world music can be especially effective choices here, or, even better try listening to music at a frequency of 750 hertz. This frequency is known as the Schumann resonance, and it is the resonant frequency of the Earth. Listening to music that vibrates at this frequency can help you to align with your true purpose in life and connect with the Earth on a deeper level.

✓ **Eat healthy foods and drink plenty of water**. Fresh fruits and vegetables, whole grains, and lean protein are packed with nutrients and antioxidants that can help keep your body healthy and your energy field clear.

✓ **The Middle Pillar Ritual** is a visualization exercise that helps to connect the energy of the different parts of the body and achieve spiritual awareness. It involves the visualization of a pillar of light extending from the crown of your head to the floor, with various other lights and colors swirling around it. This ritual can be performed at any time but is most effective when done immediately after waking up or before going to sleep.

Take a few deep breaths and relax your body as much as possible.

Focus your attention on the crown of your head and visualize a ball of white light. See this light slowly descend down the center of your body, passing through your forehead, throat, and heart. As it reaches your stomach, visualize the light splitting into two smaller balls of light, one going down each leg. When the light reaches your feet, see it coalesce back into one ball and begin to rise back up your body, passing through your heart, throat, and forehead once again.

As the light reaches the crown of your head once again, see it begin to spin and expand. Visualize it growing larger and larger until it fills your entire body with light. See the light spilling out from your body in all directions, filling the room and eventually the whole world with its light.

Once you have reached this stage, simply allow yourself to bathe in the light for as long as you like. When you are ready, slowly begin to bring your awareness back to your physical body and open your eyes.

ASTRAL PROJECTION

Astral projection is the ability to separate your consciousness from your physical body and to travel to the astral plane, the spiritual dimension that astral travelers visit during their out-of-body experiences. It is a natural ability that we all have, but most of us are not conscious of it.

Although the idea of astral travel may seem far-fetched to some, there is a growing body of evidence that suggests it can be an effective healing tool. When we are sick, our bodies are working hard to fight the disease and heal the damage. This can take a lot of energy, leaving us feeling tired and depleted. One theory is that astral travel can help to ease the burden on our physical bodies by providing a way for our consciousness to temporarily leave them behind. In this state, we can explore other realms and dimensions, free from the limitations of the physical world. This can provide a much-needed respite from the stress of illness, and allow our bodies to focus on healing. In addition, it is believed that astral travel can help us to connect with other aspects of ourselves, providing guidance and insight into our current situation.

When astral projecting, you may visit different places, meet new people or spirits, and gain insights into the nature of reality. You may also have experiences that challenge your belief system or help you to overcome fears and obstacles. The possibilities are endless. The key is to approach astral projection with an open mind and heart. Allow yourself to be open to new experiences and perspectives. Regardless of how it is achieved, astral projection can be a deeply enriching experience

Start by lying down in a comfortable position and closing your eyes.

Take some deep breaths and focus your attention on your breath.

Once you are in a deep state of relaxation, start to imagine yourself floating out of your body. Focus on the sensation of floating and let go of all other thoughts. You may feel your astral body moving through a tunnel of light.

Keep focusing on the sensation of floating.

As you inhale and exhale, feel your body becoming heavy and relaxed. Once you are in a deep state of relaxation, begin to imagine yourself floating above your body. See yourself rising through the ceiling and into the sky.

Continue upwards until you reach the stars. Then, let go and allow yourself to drift among the twinkling lights. As you float, notice any areas of your body that feel tight or in pain. These are the areas that need healing. Send light and love to these areas, and see them filled with light

You will start to observe and experience yourself from different angles and distances and you will acquire a deeper understanding of your thoughts and feelings. As you become more aware of your thoughts and feelings, you will be able to change the way you think and feel about yourself and your place in the world.

You may find your guides, angels, or spirit animals in your surroundings. If you encounter them, take a moment to listen to what they have to say.

The Astral plane is populated by spirits, and so it stands to reason that we would be able to meet our deceased loved ones there.

Look around for your loved ones. They may not look exactly as they did in life, but you will recognize them nonetheless. If you are not able to see your loved ones right away, don't worry. Just focus on their energy and feel your way around until you find them. Once you are reunited, you can spend as much time as you like catching up

You can also project your astral body out into the universe in search of your ideal partner! As you float higher and higher into the astral realms, visualize yourself moving closer and closer to your perfect mate. Envision yourself moving through the cosmos, hand-in-hand with your soulmate. When you feel you're close enough, reach out and take his/her hand. As you do, you'll begin to experience a deeper connection with this person than you ever thought possible. You may even feel like you're destined to be together. Whether you're looking for your ideal partner in this life or the next, know that the Universe is always working to bring you what you desire. All you have to do is ask and be open to receiving.

Eventually, you will start to feel your astral body becoming heavier and you will know it is time to return to your physical body. Simply focus on descending back down the staircase or ladder and feel yourself re-entering your body. Once you are back, take a few deep breaths and slowly open your eyes.

Trust that your higher self will guide you on your journey and protect you from harm. Remember, astral projection is a safe and natural phenomenon.

With a little practice, anyone can learn. So why not give it a try? Who knows where your journey might take you?

AUTOMATIC WRITING

The act of automatic writing, especially as a means of acquiring knowledge or communicating with spirits, has a long history. Supposedly, the first recorded instance of automatic writing occurred in 10th-century China. However, the practice gained popularity in the Victorian era, when people began to believe that they could use it to access hidden knowledge or contact the dead.

One of the most famous examples of automatic writing is the case of Helen Duncan a Scottish medium who was known for her ability to communicate with the dead. She allegedly used automatic writing to contact spirits and relay messages from the other side. In 1944, Helen was arrested and tried for witchcraft. The British government accused her of using automatic writing to put British soldiers in danger by relaying information about troop movements. They claimed that she could communicate with spirits and that this gave her access to secret information.

Helen was eventually found guilty and sentenced to nine months in prison. Her case remains controversial, and many people still believe that she was wrongfully convicted. To this day, some people continue to experiment with automatic writing and spiritual communication.

Automatic writing can be used to explore the subconscious mind, communicate with spirits or higher powers, and tap into hidden dimensions of reality.

Before an automatic writing session, you should cast a spell to help you focus and connect with the other side: **The Lesser Banishing Ritual of the Pentagram**

The Lesser Banishing Ritual of the Pentagram is a ceremonial magic ritual used to cleanse and protect a space and summon positive energies into your life. It can be used to banish negative energy and entities, as well as to consecrate a space for ritual work.

The ritual is performed by drawing a pentagram in each of the four cardinal directions, beginning in the east and moving clockwise. Each pentagram is inscribed with a sigil or symbol that corresponds to the element of that direction: earth in the north, the air in the east, fire in the south, and water in the west. The pentagrams are then connected by a line drawn from one point to the next, forming a continuous circle.

The magician then stands in the center of the circle and vibrates the names of God, angels, or other beings of power that correspond to the elements. This is followed by a series of invocations and blessings, after which the circle is sealed.

- *Stand facing east, in the middle of your working space.*
- *Draw a pentagram in the air with your right hand, beginning at the top point and moving downward, saying: "Ateh (אתה), Malkuth (מלכות), Geburah (גבורה), Chesed (חסד), Tiphareth (תיפארת)."*
- *Draw the same pentagram in the air with your left hand, beginning at the bottom point and moving upward, saying: "Vetah (ותה), Aralim (ארלים), Seraphim (סרפים), Malachim (מלאכים), Elohim (אלהים)."*

- *Cross your arms over your chest, left arm over right, and say: "Shaddai El Chai (שדי אל חי)."*
- *Extend your arms out to your sides at shoulder level, and say: "YHVH (יהוה), Elohim (אלהים), Tetragrammaton (תפרגממטון)."*
- *Draw a vertical line from above your head to below your feet, and say: "Michael (מיכאל), Gabriel (גבריאל), Raphael (רפאל), Uriel (אוריאל)."*
- *Now trace a circle around yourself, moving clockwise, and say: "Tzaphkiel (צפקיאל), Tzadkiel (צדקיאל), Samael (סמאל), Anael (אנאל)."*
- *Return to the east, and conclude by saying: "Amen (אמן)."*

- *Allow yourself to become completely absorbed in this visualization, clearing your mind of any other thoughts or distractions.*
- *Now sit down in a relaxed state and allow yourself to be open to whatever comes through.*
- *Write down the first thing that comes to mind, without censoring or editing yourself. Don't worry about making sense or whether the words are correct. Just let the words flow.*

You may start to experience a feeling of warmth or tingling in your hands and a sense of being directed by a higher power guiding you towards spiritual enlightenment or a greater understanding of the universe and your place within it.

1. Practice regularly, allowing yourself plenty of time to receive messages from the spirit world.

2. Set a clear intention before you begin, focusing on your goal or question and being open to all responses.

3. Pay close attention to your hand movements and any other sensations that you experience. This can help you to interpret the messages more easily.

4. Stay grounded and centered throughout the process, keeping your mind clear of distractions and focusing on receiving the message.

5. Look for patterns or recurring themes. What is being repeated?

6. Try to understand the symbolism. What do the images or words represent?

7. Consider the context. What is happening in the story or message?

8. Ask yourself what the message might mean for you.

9. Seek guidance from a trusted spiritual advisor or medium if you are having trouble interpreting what is coming through.

THE PSYCHOMANTEUM

Have you ever wished you could talk to a loved one who has passed away?

The psychomanteum is a chamber in which people can enter into a trance-like state and experience imaginary realities. It is a powerful tool for connecting with the dead, healing grief, and resolving unfinished business.

Techniques similar to psychomanteum were used by the Aztecs, who, by staring into obsidian mirrors, asked the afterlife for solutions to overcome physical, mental, and social problems. The Tibetans and Japanese also used similar methods to get in touch with more subtle dimensions of reality and receive help and support from spiritual entities.

The modern version of psychomanteum is inspired by techniques used in Ancient Greece. An oracle would get people into a semi-dark room and through prolonged observation of reflective surfaces induce them into altered states of consciousness, in which the adept could meet deceased loved ones and ask for help with problems they were facing or simply to overcome the trauma of loss.

Psychomanteum must be approached by a specialist and the following instructions are for informational purposes only.

To contact spirits in a psychomanteum, first, create the proper space:

The room should be dark and quiet, with no distractions.

Remove your shoes and any jewelry.

Once the space is prepared set up an altar in the center of the room, with a mirror placed on top. Place a candle in the center of the altar, next to the mirror, light incense on one side, and a place bowl of water on the other side.

Then, focus your attention on the mirror and say the following words:

"I summon thee, O spirits of_______. Come forth and speak with me."

Approach the spirit with reverence and respect. The spirit summoned is not a genie who will grant your every wish. Rather, it is a guide that can offer wisdom and insight into your life. The purpose of a psychomanteum is to provide a space for personal growth and spiritual exploration, not a place to ask for favors or material things from the spirits.

It is important to remember that not all spirits will be willing to communicate with you. Some may be angry, confused, or simply not ready to talk. If you encounter a spirit that is unwilling to communicate, simply thank them for their time and move on.

PENDULUM MAGIC

The use of the pendulum has been documented for millennia, from the Egyptians to Galileo and even today it continues to fascinate occult researchers, for its simplicity of use and its power.

Pendulum magic is a form of magic that uses a pendulum as a tool to focus and direct energy. A pendulum is a weight suspended from a point of support, such as a string or chain. It can be used for divination, healing, and other magical purposes. Pendulums are especially good at transmitting energy because they swing back and forth in a continuous motion. The energy is then transferred from the pendulum to your body through the process of entrainment. Entrainment is a phenomenon that occurs when two vibrating objects begin to sync up their vibrations. This happens because the vibration of one object causes the other object to start vibrating at the same frequency. When this occurs, the two objects are said to be "entrained."

Pendulums are often used in alternative medicine and healing practices. For example, some people believe that holding a pendulum over different parts of the body can help to locate areas of tension or imbalance. The pendulum has been used extensively in medieval magic and alchemy, as a way to commune with spirits or demons. In more recent times, the pendulum has been taken up by much more secular diviners, who use it as a way to access the subconscious mind or the collective unconscious.

There is no one "best" pendulum to use for divination and magic, as each individual's preferences will differ. However, some general tips on choosing a pendulum can be helpful:

- *Choose a pendulum that feels comfortable in your hand, and has a weight and size that you feel comfortable with.*
- *Try to find a pendulum made from natural materials such as wood or stone, rather than metal or plastic.*
- *If you are using the pendulum for divination, it can be helpful to choose one that is clear or pale in color.*
- *If you are using the pendulum for magic, you may want to choose one with more powerful energy, such as a black tourmaline pendulum.*

Once you have chosen your pendulum, it is important to cleanse and charge it before using it. This can be done by passing it through incense smoke or running it under cold water. Once it has been cleansed, you can start to use it.

Now you can start predicting the future by asking a series of questions and looking at the direction of the pendulum swing for each one.

> ◈ Hold it between your thumb and first two fingers, with the chain or cord hanging down, and ask the pendulum: *"Am I ready to work with you?"*

If the answer is positive go ahead and continue with the divination, otherwise, thank the pendulum and try again the next day.

Ask specific questions about what you want to know. For example, you could ask about your love life, finances, or health.

Be sure to frame your questions in a way that can be answered with a yes or no and wait for the pendulum to swing.

Once it has stopped swinging, look at the direction in which the pendulum is pointing.

-If the pendulum swings in a **clockwise direction**, this indicates a positive or affirmative answer.

-If the pendulum swings in a **counter clockwise direction**, this indicates a negative or uncertain answer.

-If the pendulum swings **back and forth in a horizontal direction**, this indicates that the question is unclear or confusing.

-If the pendulum **swings in a vertical direction**, this indicates that the question is unanswerable or irrelevant.

How to use a Pendulum to get answers from your Subconscious

- *Cast a sacred circle and call in your divine support.*

- *Hold your pendulum over a bowl of water and allow it to swing.*

- *As it swings, trace the path of the pendulum in the water with your finger.*

- *Write down what you see in the water.*

The symbols in the water represent your unconscious mind and can be interpreted by looking at their shape.

- A circle is often associated with unity or completion because it has no beginning or end.

- ❖ A square may represent stability or foundation because of its four corners.

- ❖ The triangle symbolizes balance, as it is equally weighted on all sides. It can also represent growth or expansion.

- ❖ A symbol of a snake might make us feel scared because it is associated with danger. However, the snake might also represent new beginnings or change because it sheds its skin.

Psychic attacks

Thoughts can take on a physical form and these thought-forms can influence the material world. A thought-form is a mental construct created by someone's thoughts and emotions, it's a manifestation of mental energy, much like a physical object is a manifestation of kinetic energy.

It can be either positive or negative, depending on the intention of the person creating it. It can be created deliberately by someone focusing their thoughts and energy on it, or it can be created unintentionally through strong emotions. Once created, a thoughtform will exist for as long as there is energy sustaining it. To exist, a thought-form must continuously absorb energy from its surroundings. If it does not receive enough energy, it will dissipate back into the invisibility from which it came.

A psychic attack is a deliberate and malicious attempt to harm someone using the power of thought. Psychic attacks can be used to inflict physical or mental damage, create feelings of fear or insecurity, or interfere with someone's ability to think clearly.

The intentional creation of negative thought-forms is the most common form of psychic attack, but psychic attacks can also be conducted unintentionally. Another way that psychic assaults may take place is if the attacker utilizes black magic or other dark witchcraft to put a hex on their target. This might be accomplished by casting spells, conducting rituals, or merely talking negatively about someone. Still, other ways psychic attacks may be carried out include using voodoo dolls or other objects to target the victim. The attacker may also try to send negative images through their dreams.

It is important to be aware of the power of thought forms and to protect oneself from them.

Spiritual and psychic attacks can come in many different forms, but some common signs can indicate that you are being targeted. If you are experiencing any of the following symptoms, it may be because someone is trying to hurt you:

- Feeling unusually drained of energy

- Sudden onset of negative emotions like fear, anger, or depression

- Trouble sleeping or nightmares

- Physical symptoms like headaches, stomach-aches, or unexplained pains

- You feel like you're constantly besieged by problems and difficulties, and you just can't seem to catch a break

Shielding is a psychic protection technique that involves creating an energetic barrier between yourself and another person or entity. This barrier can deflect or absorb negative energy, preventing it from reaching you. There are many different ways to create a shield, but the most important thing is to ensure that it is strong enough to block psychic attacks. Unfortunately, even the strongest shield will not be effective if it is not properly maintained. Like any other psychic protection measure, shielding requires regular attention and care to remain effective. By keeping your shield strong, you can protect yourself from psychic attacks and other negative energies. This shield can be created by visualizing a barrier of white light around you. The light should be bright enough to repel any negative energy that comes your way.

Here are some protection spells to keep you safe from harm.

- First, take a clean sheet of paper and write down the names of all the people who have ever harmed you, including anyone who has ever hurt you emotionally or physically.
- Second, fold the paper up tightly and visualize all of the negative energy being contained within it. Third, bury the paper in the ground or throw it into running water.
- Finally, say this prayer asking for protection from all forms of harm:

"Any harm that has come to me, I now release. I do not hold onto the hurt or pain of the past.
I am released from all resentment and bitterness.
All those who have harmed me are forgiven.
I blessed them and send them love. As I let go, so too am I released from any harmful patterns in my own life.
I now live in peace, surrounded by love and light.
Amen."

This spell will help to keep you safe from those who would do you harm. Repeat it as often as necessary to keep yourself protected.

Archangel Michael's shield of protection spell

The archangel Michael is one of the most powerful and well-known angels in Christianity. He is often depicted as a warrior and is the patron saint of firefighters and soldiers. In the Bible, he is described as leading God's army against Satan and his followers. Michael is also known for his role in protecting humans from harm. He can deflect negative energy and keep people safe from harm. Whether you are looking for protection from physical or spiritual harm, the Archangel Michael can be a powerful ally.

To cast the Archangel Michael shield of protection spell, you will need:

- a white candle

- a Saint Michael medal or picture

- protection oil (such as clove, sage, lavender, rosemary, or cedar)

- Light the white candle and say a prayer to Saint Michael, asking for his protection.
- Anoint yourself with the protection oil, starting at your feet and working up to your head.
- Visualize Saint Michael surrounded by a brilliant white light. See this light encircling you and protecting you from all harm.
- Repeat the following words:

"Saint Michael, surround me with your light. Keep me safe from harm and negative energy. I am protected by your love and light."

Extinguish the candle when you are finished. Carry the Saint Michael medal or picture with you, or keep it in a place of honor in your home. When we call on Michael for help, we are tapping into a powerful source of light and protection.

Archangel Camael's shield of protection spell

Camael is one of the seven archangels who stand before the throne of God. As an angel of mercy, Camael is responsible for guiding souls to the light and helping them to find peace. While Camael's primary role is to help souls transition to the afterlife, this angel also has a deep connection to the earthly realm. In particular, Camael is associated with the element of fire. As such, can be called upon for help in times of need. Whether you are facing physical or spiritual challenges, Camael is a powerful force for good that can help to protect and heal those who call upon him.

To perform the spell, you need a yellow candle and a piece of paper.

- On the paper, draw a pentacle and then write your name in the center.
- Place the paper under the candle, and light the candle.
- Visualize Camael surrounded by red light, and see him coming to stand beside you. Feel his love and protection enveloping you, and know that you are safe.
- Allow the candle to burn for as long as you feel is necessary, and then snuff it out. Keep the paper in a

safe place, and know that Camael is always with you.

Archangel Raphael's shield of protection spell

Archangel Raphael is one of the most important and well-known archangels. He is the patron saint of healers, and his name means "God heals" or "the one who helps God." Raphael is often depicted holding a medical caduceus, which is a staff with two snakes entwined around it. This symbolizes the power of healing and the ability to bring balance to both the physical and spiritual bodies. Archangel Raphael can help us to heal from physical and emotional wounds, and he can also protect us from harm and negative energies. When we call on him for help, we can feel his presence as soothing, loving energy that surrounds us and fills us with hope and peace.

As the Angel of Healing, Raphael watches over those who are ill or injured, when we call on Raphael for assistance, we can be confident that he will hear our prayers and help us to overcome whatever challenges we may be facing. Thanks to Raphael's healing power, we can experience physical, emotional, and spiritual healing in our lives.

To invoke Raphael's protection, you will need:

-A piece of green tourmaline

-Raphael's sigil (which can be found online)

- Hold the green tourmaline in your hand and focus on its calming energy.
- Visualize Raphael surrounded by a brilliant green light. See this light encircling you and protecting you from all harm.
- Repeat the following words:

"Raphael, I call on you for protection.
Surround me with your green light of healing and peace.
Keep me safe from harm and negative energy.
I am protected by your love and light."

- Carry the green tourmaline with you

Archangel Gabriel's shield of protection spell

The Archangel Gabriel is known as the "messenger of God" delivering important news or instructions to humans. In the Bible, Gabriel appeared to the Virgin Mary to announce that she would give birth to the son of God. He also appeared to the prophet Muhammad, revealing the words of the Quran. Archangel Gabriel is known as a protector and defender, and he can help us to ward off harm and negative energies. Through Gabriel's intercession, we can receive strength in times of trouble and be surrounded by love and light.

To invoke Gabriel's protection, place a white feather on your doorstep. As Gabriel is often associated with the element of air, the feather represents his presence and will help to ward off negative energy.

The Greater Banishing Ritual of the Pentagram

The Greater Banishing Ritual of the Pentagram is a powerful tool for banishing negative energy and creating a space for positive energy to flourish. This ritual can be used before or after any magical work, to help clear away any negative vibes that may have been left behind. It can also be used as a general protection ritual, to keep harmful energies at bay.

To perform the Greater Banishing Ritual of the Pentagram, you will need:

- A clean, level surface on which to draw your pentagrams
- An object for drawing (a pen, pencil)
- A bowl of water
- A bowl of salt
- An incense burner and incense

- *Start by cleaning your space. Open all the windows and doors to let in fresh air. Sweep the floors and dust the surfaces. Once your space is clean, you can begin the ritual.*
- *Draw a large pentagram. As you draw each line of the pentagram, visualize a bright white light emanating from your hand and banishing all negative energy from the space.*
- *Next, take your bowl of water and sprinkle it around the perimeter of the room, saying "I cleanse this space with water" as you do so.*
- *Then, take your bowl of salt and sprinkle it around the perimeter of the room, saying "I purify this space with salt" as you do so.*
- *Finally, light your incense and waft the smoke around the room, saying "I consecrate this space with fire" as you do so.*
- *Once you have completed all four elements of the ritual, stand in the center of your pentagram and visualize a bright white light emanating from your body and filling the entire space. Feel the positive energy of the space fill you up and banish all negative thoughts and emotions*

from your mind.

- *Stay in this meditative state for as long as you feel comfortable, then open your eyes and begin your magical work.*

The Rose Cross Ritual

The Rose Cross Ritual is a ceremonial magic ritual used to invoke the power of the rose and the cross. It is said to be a powerful protective ritual that can shield you from harm.

Cast a circle around yourself and light a white candle.

Stand in the center of the circle and say the following:

- *"Oh, Great Divine Spirit, I ask for your protection and guidance as I perform this ritual. I consecrate myself to your service and ask that you bless me with your power and love. So mote it be."*

Trace a pentagram in the air with your right hand, starting at the lower left point and ending at the top point. As you trace the pentagram, say:

- *"I invoke thee, oh great Archangel Michael, to protect me as I work my magic."*

Trace a pentagram in the air with your left hand, starting at the lower right point and ending at the top point. As you trace the pentagram, say:

- *"I invoke thee, oh great Archangel Raphael, to heal me as I work my magic."*

Place your right hand over your heart and your left hand over your groin, and say:

- *"I invoke thee, oh great Archangel Uriel, to enlighten me as I work my magic."*

With both hands, trace a cross in the air, starting at the top point and ending at the bottom point. As you trace the cross, say:

- *"I invoke thee, oh great Archangel Gabriel, to inspire me as I work my magic."*

Now trace a rose in the air with your right hand, starting at the center and spiraling outwards. As you trace the rose, say:

- *"I invoke thee, oh Great Mother Goddess, to fill me with your love and light."*

Finally, trace a pentagram in the air with your left hand, starting at the lower left point and ending at the top point. As you trace the pentagram, say:

- *"I invoke thee, oh great Horned God, to give me strength and courage as I work my magic."*

Take a deep breath and feel the energies of the Archangels and the Gods flow through you. Say the following:

- *"I am now surrounded by a column of white light, which protects me from all harm. I am safe, I am loved, I am protected. So mote it be."*

Extinguish the candle and open the circle.

Crystals

When it comes to psychic attacks, there are a few crystals that can help provide protection. One of the most useful is **black tourmaline**, which is known for its ability to deflect negative energy. It can also be helpful to keep a piece of **obsidian** on hand, as it can help to block outside energies from entering your auric field. **Citrine** is another good option, as it helps to dissolve negative thought patterns and clear away any residual energy from past trauma. **Lapis lazuli** helps to open our Third Eye chakra and deepen our connection to our intuition, this allows us to see clearly what is happening around us and make choices from a place of inner knowing. **Hematite** is particularly effective at groundings us and keeping us rooted in the present moment, which can be very helpful when we are feeling overwhelmed by outside forces.

Once you have chosen your crystals, cleanse them and charge them with your intention to create a protective barrier.

Then, place them at the six points of the compass around your property. Some people like to bury the crystals in the ground, while others simply set them on the ground or a windowsill. If you are using buried crystals, it is important to mark their locations so that you can retrieve them later. As you place each crystal, visualize it creating a shield of light that repels negative energy and protects your home from harm.

If you find yourself under regular psychic attack, it may be worthwhile to invest in a piece of protective jewelry made with one or more of these crystals, by wearing or carrying these stones, we can create a barrier between ourselves and the negativity that surrounds us.

Psychic attacks can come in the form of thoughts, words, or deeds that are intended to cause harm. They can also be the result of toxic relationships or situations that drain our energy and leave us feeling depleted but It's important to realize that your thoughts are just as powerful as anyone else's.

SCRYING

Scrying is a form of divination that uses a mirror or other reflective surface to view things from the perspective of spirits. The word scrying comes from the Old English "descry," which means "to reveal." The first recorded use of scrying was in the 1st century by the Greek physician Galen, who used it to diagnose illnesses. Scrying was then popularized in the Victorian era by occultists and spiritualists who used it as a way to commune with the dead. This form of divination soon became popular throughout Europe and was used by many famous occultists including Nostradamus and Aleister Crowley. Today, it is still practiced by many people all over the world.

Different scrying tools can be used, but some of the most popular include crystal balls, black mirrors, and scrying bowls. Each tool has its unique properties that can help you access different information.

Choose your scrying tool.

- Crystal balls are thought to be one of the most powerful scrying tools. They help amplify your psychic abilities and connect you with your higher self.
- Black mirrors help see into the future, as they allow you to peer into the depths of your subconscious mind.
- Scrying bowls can be used to scry in water, water is associated with emotions it helps you access your

feelings and intuition.

Cleanse your scrying tool.

Once you've chosen your scrying tool, it's important to cleanse it before use. This will help to clear away any negative energy that might be attached to it. You can cleanse your scrying tool by holding it under running water or smudging it with sage.

Prepare yourself mentally and emotionally.

Before scrying, it's important to prepare yourself mentally and emotionally. This means taking a few deep breaths and relaxing your mind and body. It's also helpful to set an intention for your scrying session. Focus on a specific question or issue that you're hoping to get guidance on.

Begin scrying

- *Write down your question or what you would like guidance on in the middle of the piece of paper.*
- *Fold the paper three times towards you and then tie it with a pink ribbon.*
- *Place a candle in front of you and light it.*
- *Hold an amethyst crystal in your non-dominant hand and focus on your question.*
- *Visualize a pink light surrounding you and infusing you with clairvoyant power.*
- *Say aloud, "I open my third eye to see clearly what lies ahead."*

Once you're feeling mentally and emotionally prepared, it's time to begin scrying. Start by holding your scrying tool in front of you and gazing into its surface. Relax your eyes and allow your gaze to soften. You may see colors, shapes, or symbols begin to emerge. Allow whatever images come to you to flow freely.

*7. **Interpret your visions.***

Once you have finished scrying, take some time to interpret the images and messages you received. It's important to trust your intuition as you interpret these visions, as they can be quite symbolic. With practice, you will get better at scrying and begin to receive more clear and concise messages.

Look at them as metaphors for your life. For example, if you see a snake in your scrying tool, you might take that to mean that someone is being "slippery" with you and not being truthful. If you see a rose in your scrying tool, you might interpret that as meaning love and beauty are coming into your life.

Snakes are also seen as symbols of transformation. Seeing a snake in your scrying tool might mean that you are about to go through a major change in your life.

Horses are symbols of strength and power. Seeing a horse in your scrying tool might mean that you need to tap into those qualities to achieve something.

Roses are symbols of love and beauty. Seeing a rose in your scrying tool might represent the coming of good things into your life.

Crows: are harbingers of bad news, so seeing them in your scrying tool might mean that difficult times are ahead.

Stars represent your hopes and dreams for the future.

Eagles are associated with strength and courage. Seeing one in your scrying tool might mean that you need to tap into those qualities to overcome a challenge.

Circles are often seen as symbols of completion or wholeness. Seeing a circle in your scrying tool might represent coming full circle in your life or resolving a situation.

Trees are often seen as symbols of growth and life. Seeing a tree in your scrying tool might represent a new beginning or a fresh start.

During your session, you may also see pentacles, cups, swords, and wands. Each one of these symbols represents an element of the scrying session. The pentacle is a symbol of magic itself. The cups represent the emotions and experiences that are seen in the scrying session. Swords represent the thoughts and ideas that come to mind during the scrying. Wands represent the creative power and potential that is available during the session.

These symbols may appear in any order or combination during a scrying session. They are used to give guidance and understanding to the scryer about what they are seeing.

Once you have finished scrying, take some time to interpret the images and messages you received. It's important to trust your intuition as you interpret these visions, as they can be quite symbolic. With practice, you will get better at scrying and begin to receive more clear and concise messages. Pay attention to your dreams as well, as they may offer additional clues about the meaning of your visions.

CRYSTAL BALL

A crystal ball also known as an orbuculum is a spherical object that is used as a tool for divination and fortune-telling. The earliest known use of crystal balls dates back to the 6th century AD, when they were used by Celtic tribes for scrying, or seeing into the future. Crystal balls have been used throughout history by many different cultures for a variety of purposes. In the Middle Ages, they were believed to be able to reveal a person's thoughts and feelings and were often used as a means of communication with spirits. Today, crystal balls are still used for divination and fortune-telling and are thought to be able to channel positive energy and promote relaxation.

The ball is to be able to focus and amplify one's thoughts and energy, making it easier to reach out to otherworldly beings. Some believe that the ball itself is alive and has a consciousness, while others see it as nothing more than a conduit.

There are a few things to keep in mind when using a crystal ball for contact spirits. First, it is important to be respectful of the ball and the spirits. Second, it is necessary to focus your thoughts and energy on the task at hand. And finally, it is helpful to have an intention or question in mind before beginning. With these things in mind, the experience of contacting spirits through a crystal ball can be both profound and enlightening.

- First, find a quiet spot where you will not be disturbed.

- Then, sit down and relax, taking a few deep breaths.
- Once you are feeling calm, hold the crystal ball in your hands and focus your attention on it. Visualize a white light emanating from the ball and entering your body.
- Feel the light filling you with peace and tranquility. Now, begin to think about the spirit you wish to contact.
- Picture them in your mind and send them a message of love and goodwill.
- Hold the intention of connecting with that spirit in your heart, and see if you can sense their presence in the crystal ball.
- You may see their face appear, or receive a mental image of them. Just let whatever comes up flow through you without judgment.

After a few minutes, thank the spirit for connecting with you and say goodbye. Once you are finished, take some time to journal about your experience. Did you feel the presence of the spirit? Did they communicate with you in any way? What did you learn from the experience? Remember, there are no wrong answers – just trust your intuition and go with what feels right for you.

ESSENTIAL OILS

If you're interested in developing your psychic abilities, there are a few essential oils that can help. Whether you're just getting started on your psychic journey or you've been at it for a while, incorporating these essential oils into your practice can give you a boost.

Rosemary oil

Rosemary oil has myriad benefits, one of which is enhancing memory and recall. This can be helpful not only in remembering your dreams but also in accessing memories from past lives. In the world of mediumship, rosemary is often used as a tool to help facilitate contact with the departed. The herb is said to open the mind and heart, making it easier to receive messages from the other side. When used in this way, rosemary can be a powerful tool for gaining insights into our past lives.

Peppermint oil

As anyone who has ever taken a whiff of peppermint oil knows, the scent is refreshing and invigorating. But did you know that peppermint oil can also help to improve concentration and focus? This makes it an ideal tool for use in mediumship and psychic development. When you are trying to tune into your intuition, it can be helpful to have a clear mind, and peppermint oil can help with that. Simply put a few drops on a cloth or diffuser and breathe in the fresh, minty aroma.

Clary sage oil decrease anxiety and promotes relaxation, both of which are conducive to increased Psychic awareness. Clary sage sharpens the senses and opens the third eye, making it easier to receive messages from beyond. Whether you're looking to deepen your understanding of the afterlife or simply seeking a more relaxed state of mind, clary sage may be worth a try.

Sandalwood oil

The woody, sweet scent of sandalwood increases clarity and promotes inner peace, making it ideal for meditation and prayer. Sandalwood oil encourages spiritual connection and communication with other realms.

Jasmine oil

The scent of jasmine is uplifting and relaxing, making it easier to reach a state of trance. Jasmine oil helps open the third eye chakra; When used before a reading, can help to clear the mind and open the channels of communication between the medium and the spirits and It can be used to create an atmosphere of peace and calm, which can be helpful in raising one's vibration and attracting benevolent spirits.

Neroli oil

Neroli oil eases anxiety and promotes mental clarity, making it an ideal tool for those seeking to develop their psychic abilities. In addition, neroli oil encourages communication with the spirit world and facilitates contact with loved ones who have passed on. For many people, using neroli oil is a way to connect with the other side and to gain insight into the workings of the universe.

Ylang-ylang oil

The Ylang-ylang oil is extracted from the flowers of the ylang-ylang tree, which is native to Southeast Asia. The tree is often used in traditional ceremonies and is believed to have spiritual powers. Ylang-ylang oil has a sweet, floral scent and It is used in aromatherapy to promote relaxation and blissful sleep. Ylang-ylang oil promotes happiness, peace, well-being, and psychic visions.

CONCLUSION

Psychic abilities are not a hoax, as many people believe. The ability to see beyond the veil of the physical world and into the spiritual realm is a real and natural ability that we all possess. However, for most of us, this ability remains dormant. Through proper instruction and practice, however, anyone can learn. If you feel called to develop your psychic abilities, I encourage you to follow the steps outlined in this book and seek out further instruction from a qualified teacher.

About the Author

My path as a spiritual author and intuitive guide began in my childhood when I discovered a passion for exploring mystical symbols and traditions beyond the confines of mainstream belief systems. After university, I deepened my studies of esoteric wisdom and ancient divination practices during extended stays at spiritual communities abroad.

Today I blend scholarly research of metaphysical topics with hands-on guidance rooted in over a decade of professional experience. My passion is helping fellow seekers cultivate an intimate relationship with their intuition to unlock deeper fulfillment, self-understanding and purpose.

Milton Keynes UK
Ingram Content Group UK Ltd.
UKHW050816250324
439991UK00001B/56